Telling th

A Passover Haggadah
Explained

adapted by Barry Louis Polisar

with illustrations by Sierra Hannah Polisar

The Haggadah was originally designed to help people understand and appreciate the significance of the Passover story but Haggadot can be confusing to those not familiar with the holiday traditions. I felt there was a need for a simple, basic Haggadah that would keep with the traditional order of the night – and also follow the Torah commandment to "tell the story." I also wanted to give a little more background on why we do what we do each year to help re-connect with the original spiritual reasons that gave birth to our traditions.

The Haggadah is in itself a ritualized retelling of the Passover story, and through the years it has been adapted and changed. Though originally written in Hebrew and Aramaic, Rabbis urged that the story be told in a language that would be accessible to all. There is a long tradition of finding new ways to recount the story of the exodus in order to make it more engaging to those at the Seder table but sometimes, the symbolism and significance of the holiday is sacrificed in the retelling. This Haggadah, illustrated by my daughter, is presented with the hope that readers and families will be encouraged to add their own traditions and make this story a living one that evolves and becomes more meaningful each year.

BLP

Illustrations © by Sierra Hannah Polisar
Typography and design by Chris Abshire

My Grandmother's father Louis had a story he used to tell. It was about God giving the Jewish people religion, and my Grandmother told the story to me when I was young: "It's really not such a hard religion," God said. "Here, I'll write it down for you. You try it for a while and if it doesn't suit you, bring it back." So the Jewish people tried it and found it was too hard. For days, caravan upon caravan stretched across the desert carrying haftorahs, mezuzahs, yarmulkes, prayer shawls, commentaries and prayer books. God looked out at the caravans that stretched to the horizon and said, "What's all this? All I wrote down for you were ten simple commandments."

Of course, I now realize there is more to Judaism than the story of the ten commandments. The full story is actually many, many stories – rich with history, irony, and lessons for our own lives.

There is another story that has guided me; a Hassidic tale about a Rabbi who saw that his village was about to be attacked. He went into a special part of the forest, lit a fire, and said a prayer so that his village might be spared. A generation later, when another threat was upon the village, another Rabbi would go to the same place in the forest and light a fire... but he did not know the prayer. Still later, another Rabbi, hoping to save his people once more, would go into the forest. He did not know the prayer – or even how to light the fire. Finally, in another generation, there was another threat and another Rabbi. He was unable to light the fire, he did not know the prayer; and he couldn't even find the place in the forest. When I first heard that story, I realized that without a deliberate effort, our Jewish heritage might become so diminished that soon, we would be unable to say the prayers, light the fire, or find our own place in the forest.

Stories shape our lives and the story of Passover is one that has been passed down through the generations. We retell it every year and as we retell it, we discover new meaning for ourselves in the story.

Barry Louis Polisar

3

WE OBSERVE

Tonight, as we gather together among family and friends, we observe an ancient festival that recalls the slavery of our people and their deliverance out of bondage. Through the ages, Jews have commemorated the Exodus in order to remember that our ancestors were once slaves in the land of Egypt.

We are not the only people to have been enslaved by others. The Passover Seder reminds us that in every age we must all do whatever we can to help those who are enslaved by tyranny. If a people is anywhere enslaved, exploited or oppressed, then nowhere is freedom really secure. And freedom must never be taken for granted.

This Seder is not just a series of prayers to be said quickly in order to get to the meal. It is a ritual that connects us to our past. The Seder – which means "order" – consists of fifteen different steps; over time, additional customs, songs and hymns have been added. A Seder Plate with specific foods is prepared before the meal and all bread and leavened products are removed from the home before the holiday begins to fulfill the Torah commandment that during this week of observance "no leaven shall be found in your homes." Each year, we are encouraged to discover new things in the Seder so that in every generation, each one of us will feel as if he or she "came forth" out of Egypt. It is in this spirit that the story is told and handed down, each generation knowing it has the responsibility to tell the story to the next generation.

LIGHTING THE FESTIVAL CANDLES

Our holiday begins just before sundown with the lighting of two candles accompanied by a blessing. On Friday night, an additional blessing is added for the Sabbath. Though these prayers were traditionally said by the mother of the house, there is no reason we cannot all join in the prayer together:

בָּרוּךְ אַתָּה יהוה אֱלֹהֵינוּ מֶלֶךְ הָעוֹלָם אֲשֶׁר קִדְּשָׁנוּ
בְּמִצְוֹתָיו וְצִוָּנוּ לְהַדְלִיק נֵר שֶׁל יוֹם טוֹב.

**Baruch Atah Adonai, Eloheinu Melech ha-olam,
asher kidishanu b'mitzvohsov, vitzivanu la-had-lek ner shel yom tov.**

Blessed art Thou our Lord, our God, King of the universe, who hast sanctified us by giving us your commandments and granting us the privilege of kindling these holiday candles.

May this coming year be a year of health and goodness for our friends and family and for all people. May these Holiday candles bring peace within our souls, goodness and cheer within our hearts, and happiness within our families and in our homes as it spreads its light on each of us.

בָּרוּךְ אַתָּה יהוה אֱלֹהֵינוּ מֶלֶךְ הָעוֹלָם שֶׁהֶחֱיָנוּ
וְקִיְּמָנוּ וְהִגִּיעָנוּ לַזְּמַן הַזֶּה.

**Baruch Atah Adonai, Eloheinu Melech ha-olam, she-heh-che-yanu,
v'ki-y'manu, v'higi-anu lazman hazeh.**

Blessed art Thou, O Lord, our God, King of the Universe, who has granted us life, sustained us, and brought us to this festive season. We thank thee O Lord for the blessings of life and of health. We pray that the coming year will be a year of happiness and peace.

TOGETHER

On this night we retell the story of the Exodus from slavery in Egypt, just as our people have done for thousands of years. We share these rituals with our children because it is written, "You shall keep the Feast of Unleavened Bread, for on this very day I brought you out of bondage. You shall observe this day throughout the generations as a practice for all times."

The Torah commands us to tell our children about the Exodus from Egypt, and the first night of Passover is to be a "night of watching." In earlier times the Israelites fulfilled these requirements by staying up all night retelling the story. "Haggadah", which means "telling", does just that; it tells the story of the Exodus.

The Torah states that Passover should be observed for seven days. After the exile from Judea, when Jews lived in countries throughout the world, an extra day was added because of the uncertainty of the calendar. Today, many Jews observe the holiday for eight days while others follow the Israeli practice of observing the holiday for seven days as prescribed in the Torah.

fill the first cup of wine

Wine gladdens the heart. The Torah tells us four times to recount the story of our redemption from slavery and we will drink wine four times during the course of this Seder while reclining; twice before the meal and twice after the meal. Wine is a symbol of joy and happiness and we thank God that we are able to gather together again with friends and family to observe this Festival just as our ancestors have done for centuries.

Raise wine glasses and recite the following together before drinking:

בָּרוּךְ אַתָּה יהוה אֱלֹהֵינוּ מֶלֶךְ הָעוֹלָם בּוֹרֵא פְּרִי הַגָּפֶן.

Baruch Atah Adonai, Eloheinu Melech ha-olam, borei p'ri ha-gafen.

Praised be thou, O Lord Our God, King of the Universe, who has created the fruit of the vine!

You have called us for service from among the peoples and have hallowed our lives with commandments. You have given us festivals for rejoicing, seasons of celebration, this Festival of Freedom, a day of sacred assembly commemorating the Exodus from bondage.

In the Passover story, God promises deliverance four times: "I will take you out from under the burdens of Egypt; and I will deliver you from their bondage; I will redeem you with an outstretched arm and with great judgments; and I will take you to Me for a people." As we drink the first of four cups of wine, we thank God for giving us life, for sustaining us, and allowing us to reach this moment. We know that life is fragile. Each day is a gift to be cherished and no moment should be taken for granted. We thank God for helping us maintain a life of meaning and we are thankful for having opportunities to sanctify our lives by performing good deeds that make a difference in the world.

All drink the first cup of wine

U-R'HATZ - Washing the Hands

Washing hands is done before all meals and water plays an important part in the Passover story. We wash our hands twice at our Seder, but since we will not be eating yet, we do not recite any blessings at this time. As we pour water over our hands now, we ask that our hearts be touched by wisdom as our hands reach out to the world and touch those around us.

A pitcher of water may be passed around to all guests

In ancient times our people were farmers and shepherds. In this festive season, we are meant to feel a connection with the food we eat from the land and to remember that we are surrounded by blessings and miracles no less majestic than those our ancestors witnessed thousands of years ago. Spring reminds us that we are again given a chance for renewal; a new chance to create peace and goodness in our world. We dip karpas – greens – to symbolize this renewal. The salt water symbolizes the bitter tears shed by our ancestors in slavery.

Each person takes greens, dips them in salt water and recites the following:

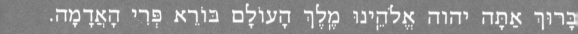

בָּרוּךְ אַתָּה יהוה אֱלֹהֵינוּ מֶלֶךְ הָעוֹלָם בּוֹרֵא פְּרִי הָאֲדָמָה.

Baruch Atah Adonai, Eloheinu Melech ha-olam, borei p'ri ha-adamah.

**We praise You, Adonai, Sovereign of Life,
Who creates the fruit of the earth.**

Eat the Karpas

YAHATZ - Break the Middle Matzoh

We read in the Torah: "It is commanded that you should eat unleavened bread and for seven days there shall be no leavened bread seen with you. And you shall tell your children in that day, saying, 'This is done because of that which God did to me when I came forth out of Egypt for with a strong hand has God brought you out of Egypt.' You shall keep this ordinance in its season from year to year."

There is a tradition of searching for additional meaning in the text of the Torah. Since the Hebrew scrolls were written without vowels, Rabbis have read the commandment, "You shall observe the feast of Matzoh" and realized that by changing some of the letters, the word "matzoh" becomes "mitzvoh." A mitzvoh is a commandment. But the word also means a good deed and we are meant to link our rituals with doing good in the world.

On Sabbaths and holidays, we traditionally have two loaves of bread, a symbol of the double portion of "manna from heaven." On Passover, we have three matzot on the table; the third matzoh is the "bread of affliction." We now take the middle of the three matzot and break it in two. By breaking "bread" we signify hospitality and invite all who are hungry to join us. The smaller piece of matzoh is replaced between the other two matzot. The larger piece is wrapped in a napkin – symbolic of our ancestors wrapping their dough in their garments when they departed Egypt – and set aside as the "afikomen" to be eaten after the meal. Together we say the words which join us with our people and with all who are in need.

All recite these words:

Behold the Matzoh, bread of poverty which our ancestors ate in the land of Egypt. This is the bread of affliction, the bread our ancestors ate as slaves in the land of Egypt.

Let all who are hungry come and eat. Let all who are needy share the hope of this Passover celebration.

Next year may all men and women be free.

The wine glasses are refilled

THE FOUR QUESTIONS

Questioning is a healthy sign of freedom. Asking questions is so fundamental that, according to the rabbis, even if one finds oneself alone on Passover, the Four Questions should be asked aloud.

Traditionally, the youngest child is called upon to ask these four questions about the differences that mark this night. We encourage children to question and all who are present may ask the Four Questions.

מַה נִּשְׁתַּנָּה הַלַּיְלָה הַזֶּה מִכָּל הַלֵּילוֹת.

שֶׁבְּכָל הַלֵּילוֹת אָנוּ אוֹכְלִין חָמֵץ וּמַצָּה,
הַלַּיְלָה הַזֶּה כֻּלּוֹ מַצָּה.
שֶׁבְּכָל הַלֵּילוֹת אָנוּ אוֹכְלִין שְׁאָר יְרָקוֹת,
הַלַּיְלָה הַזֶּה מָרוֹר.
שֶׁבְּכָל הַלֵּילוֹת אֵין אָנוּ מַטְבִּילִין אֲפִילוּ פַּעַם אֶחָת,
הַלַּיְלָה הַזֶּה שְׁתֵּי פְעָמִים.
שֶׁבְּכָל הַלֵּילוֹת אָנוּ אוֹכְלִין בֵּין יוֹשְׁבִין וּבֵין מְסֻבִּין,
הַלַּיְלָה הַזֶּה כֻּלָּנוּ מְסֻבִּין.

Ma nish-ta-na ha-lyla ha-zeh meekol ha-laila?

She-be-chol ha-lay-lot anu ochlin chamaytz u-matzo,
ha-laila ha-zeh kulo matzo

She-be-chol ha-lay-lot anu ochlin sh'or y'rokot,
ha-laila ha-zeh maror

She-be-chol ha-lay-lot ayn anu mat-beeleen afeelu pa-am e-chat
ha-laila ha-zeh shatay f'amim

She-be-chol ha-lay-lot anu ochlin bayn yoshvin u-vayn m'subin
ha-laila ha-zeh kulanu m'subin

Why is this night different from all other nights?

On all other nights, we eat either leavened bread or matzoh;
why, on this night do we eat only matzoh?

On all other nights, we eat all kinds of herbs;
why, on this night, do we especially eat bitter herbs?

On all other nights, we do not dip herbs at all;
why, on this night, do we dip them twice?

On all other nights, we eat in an ordinary manner;
why, tonight, do we recline and dine with a special ceremony?

FOUR ANSWERS

Later, we will read and explore the whole story of the Exodus from Egypt, but first we give a simple answer to each of these four questions.

We eat matzoh because when our ancestors were told by Pharaoh that they could leave Egypt, they had no time to allow their bread to rise, so they baked hurriedly, without leavening.

At the Seder, we eat bitter herbs to remind us of the bitterness our ancestors experienced when they were oppressed as slaves.

At the Seder table, we dip food twice; once in salt water to remind us of the tears shed in slavery and again in haroset, to remind us that there is sweetness even in bitter times.

In ancient times, slaves ate hurriedly, standing or squatting on the ground. Symbolically, as a sign of freedom, we lean and relax as we partake of wine and symbolic food.

The Haggadah tells the story of Rabbi Akiba and other Talmudic scholars sitting at the Seder table in B'nai B'rak all night long discussing the events of the liberation from Egypt. They talked all night until their students came in to announce it was time for the morning prayers. If great scholars can find the theme of freedom so fascinating that it keeps them up all night, our Seder too, will be made more interesting with questions, comments and discussion on this theme.

THE FOUR CHILDREN

Four times the Torah commands us to tell our children about the Exodus from Egypt and because of this, traditional Haggadot speak of four kinds of sons. The Hebrew word for "children" is the same word as "sons" and either can be used. Our sages teach that perhaps there is really a part of each of the four children in us all.

The wise child questions, "What is the meaning of the laws and observances which the Lord, our God, has commanded?" In response to this child we explain the observances of the Passover in-depth.

The scornful child questions, "What does this service mean to you?" This child says "to you" and does not feel a part of our observances. By excluding himself, this child would not have been redeemed had he or she been in Egypt. We ask this child to listen closely and become part of our traditions and learn what the Seder means.

The simple child questions, "What is this ceremony about?" We say, "We are remembering a time long ago when we were forced to work as slaves. God made us a free people and we are celebrating our freedom." We hope by observing the Seder year after year, this child will come to appreciate the message of the Passover holiday.

The innocent child doesn't think to question. To this child we say, "In the spring of every year we remember how we were brought out of slavery to freedom."

Rabbis in the Lubovitch tradition remind us that there is also a fifth child... the one who is not at this table. This is the person who should be with us, but is not... and we mark his absence.

There is a word in Hebrew – Teshuvah – that means return. It is an acknowledgement that there is always a chance for forgiveness, redemption and change. Our traditions provide that Passover is open to all. Everyone is welcome at this table. There is always room. Because no one is ever turned away, there is always an opportunity for a rebirth of spirit.

As a sign of hospitality to all, we open the door to our homes and symbolically invite anyone who wants to join us to come inside.

At this point, the children open the door

WE WERE SLAVES

The Haggadah sets forth the theme that we – not just our ancestors – were slaves to Pharaoh but God delivered each of us "with a mighty hand and an outstretched arm." We tell the story of the Exodus and search its meaning to better understand and appreciate its message.

We have an obligation to retell and expand upon the story of our Exodus from Egypt in order to remind ourselves that the struggle for freedom is a constant one. Over the years, Rabbis reasoned that since the Torah commands us to retell the story, this must be done creatively, in a way that is compelling to the next generation. The Torah directs us to say, "My father was a wandering Aramean," but traditional Haggadot translate the verse as "The Aramean wanted to destroy my father." This was done as a warning to be on guard against two types of enemies who would take away our freedom – the enemy without and the enemy within, posing as a friend and betraying us.

We are also asked to be mindful of two kinds of slavery: physical bondage and spiritual bondage. We must strive to be free in body, but also free in spirit, careful not to destroy ourselves and our people by turning from God and the faith of our ancestors. Throughout the ages, our people have been oppressed and attacked by outside forces, but there is an equal risk of destroying ourselves by abandoning our traditions and repudiating who we are.

All raise their cups of wine, but do not drink

In every generation men rise up against us, seeking to destroy us, and in every generation God delivers us from their hands into freedom.

All replace their cups untasted

MAGGID - The Story

The Torah says we are to speak these words before God and say, "My father was a wandering Aramean. He went down into Egypt and sojourned there. With few in number, he became there a great and populous nation. The Egyptians dealt harshly with us and afflicted us and imposed hard labor upon us. And we cried out to the Lord, the God of our fathers and God heard our cry and saw our affliction and our oppression. He brought us out of Egypt with a mighty hand and with an outstretched arm and with great signs and wonders."

We will now recount the Passover story. As we read, we will go around the table with each person taking a turn to read a paragraph out loud:

Our patriarch Abraham and his wife Sarah went to the land of Canaan, where he became the founder of "a great nation." God tells Abraham, "Know this for certain, that your descendants will be strangers in a strange land, and be enslaved and oppressed for four hundred years. But know that in the end I shall bring judgment on the oppressors."

Abraham's Grandson, Jacob and his family went down to Egypt during a time of famine throughout the land. In Egypt, Jacob and the Israelites lived and prospered until a new Pharaoh arose who said, "Behold the children of Israel are too many and too mighty for us. Let us then deal shrewdly with them, lest they become more powerful, and in the event of war, join our enemies in fighting against us and gain control over the region."

The Egyptians set taskmasters over the Israelites with forced labor and made them build cities for Pharaoh. The Egyptians embittered the lives of the Israelites with harsh labor but the more they were oppressed, the more they increased and the Egyptians came to despise them. Pharaoh ordered, "Every Hebrew boy that is born shall be thrown in the Nile River and drowned."

God remembered the covenant that he made with Abraham and Sarah and called to Moses, telling him to appear before Pharaoh and demand that the Hebrew people be released from bondage. But Pharaoh refused to free the Israelites. Nine times Moses and his brother Aaron went to Pharaoh, and each time that Pharaoh refused Moses' request, God sent a plague to Egypt.

After the ninth plague, Moses summoned the elders of Israel, and said to them, "Draw out lambs for your families. Take a bunch of hyssop, and dip it in the blood that is in the basin, and strike the lintel and the two side posts with the blood that is in the basin; and none of you shall go out at the door of his house until the morning. For God will pass through to smite the Egyptians; and when he sees the blood upon the lintel, and on the two side posts, God will pass over the door, and will not suffer the destroyer to come in to your houses to smite you."

It is written in the Torah that God hardened the heart of Pharaoh during Moses' pleas. Finally when God brought down the tenth plague upon them – the death of the first-born of all the Egyptians – a great cry went up through-out Egypt, and Pharaoh allowed Moses to take his people out of the land and deliver them to a new land.

It is written: "And it shall come to pass, when you come to the land which God will give you, according as he has promised, that you shall keep this service. And it shall come to pass, when your children shall say to you, "What mean you by this service?" you shall say, it is the sacrifice of God's Passover, who passed over the houses of the children of Israel in Egypt."

As Moses and the Israelites were fleeing Egypt, Pharaoh's armies pursued them as they were encamped by the sea. Moses held out his hand over the sea and the Lord drove back the sea, allowing the Israelites to pass dry shod, but drowned the Egyptians.

There is a Midrash that tells of God rebuking his angels for rejoicing as the Egyptians were drowning, saying, "Are these not my children also?"

We now pour ten drops of wine to symbolize the ten plagues upon Egypt. A full cup of wine is the symbol of complete joy. Though we celebrate our freedom, our cup cannot be filled because our freedom did not come without a cost. Each drop of wine that we pour out of our cups diminishes our joy.

THE TEN PLAGUES

With your finger or spoon, lessen your cup of wine with each of the plagues mentioned, but do not drink

Blood as we read "All the waters that were in the river were turned to blood"

Frogs as we read "And the frogs came up, and covered the land of Egypt"

Lice as we read "All the dust of the land became lice throughout all of Egypt"

Swarms as we read "There came a grievous swarm of flies into the house of Pharaoh, and into his servants' houses, and into all the land of Egypt."

Pestilence as we read "All the cattle of Egypt died."

Boils as we read "And they took ashes of the furnace, and stood before Pharaoh; and Moses sprinkled it up toward heaven; and it became a boil breaking forth with blains upon man, and upon beast."

Hail as we read "And Moses stretched forth his rod toward heaven: and God sent thunder and hail, and the fire ran along upon the ground; and God rained hail upon the land of Egypt.

Locusts as we read "And Moses stretched forth his rod over the land of Egypt, and God brought an east wind upon the land all that day, and all that night; and when it was morning, the east wind brought the locusts."

Darkness as we read "And Moses stretched forth his hand toward heaven; and there was a thick darkness in all the land of Egypt three days."

The death of the Egyptian first-born as we read "And it came to pass, that at midnight God smote all the firstborn in the land of Egypt."

It is interesting to note that the last thing God does against Pharaoh is the first thing that Pharaoh does to the Israelites, a lesson that we should not be vengeful and always have measured justice. "An eye for an eye" does not mean we should seek equal retribution, but that when pursuing justice, we must be fair and equitable. Even as we recount the Passover story, the Torah instructs us to "not abhor the Egyptian."

At this time, we are reminded to be aware of the plagues that afflict us in the world about us – and in the relationships we share with others. God sent ten plagues but he also gave us ten commandments to live by. If we abide by these commandments, we can remove many of the plagues from our lives and from our hearts.

DAYENU - it would have been enough

A Medieval addition to the Haggadah, this hymn originally contained fifteen verses mirroring the fifteen steps in the Seder.

How many are the gifts God bestowed upon us!

Had God:

Brought us out of Egypt and not divided the sea for us,	**Dayenu**
Divided the sea and not permitted us to cross on dry land,	**Dayenu**
Permitted us to cross on dry land and not sustained us for forty years in the desert,	**Dayenu**
Sustained us for forty years in the desert and not fed us with manna,	**Dayenu**
Fed us with manna and not given us the Sabbath,	**Dayenu**
Given us the Sabbath and not brought us to Mount Sinai,	**Dayenu**
Brought us to Mount Sinai and not given us the Torah,	**Dayenu**

Day, Dayenu, day, dayenu, day, dayenu, dayenu, dayenu dayenu...

**Ilu hotsi hotsianu, hotsianu mi-Mitzrayim,
hotisanu mi-Mitzrayim, Dayenu
Ilu natan natan lanu, natan lanu et ha-Shabot,
natan lanu et ha-Shabot, Dayenu.
Ilu natan natan lanu, natan lanu et ha-Torah,
natan lanu et ha-Torah, Dayenu.**

PESACH, MATZOH, MAROR

Pesach, matzoh, and maror have symbolic meaning for us. They are so important and so meaningful that no Seder is really complete unless they are fully explained.

WHAT IS THE MEANING OF THIS PESACH?

This roasted shank bone is the symbol of the Pesach lamb. Each year at Passover, the Israelites would gather at the Temple to commemorate the Exodus from slavery. Each family would bring a lamb as an offering, to remember the time when our ancestors were spared the fate of the Egyptians. The Pesach was a reminder that God passed over the houses of our ancestors in Egypt. Originally, one of the four questions asked at the Seder was not, "Why do we recline?" but "Why do we eat only roasted meat?" After the Temple was destroyed, sacrifices were abandoned and so was the question about eating only roasted meats at the Seder.

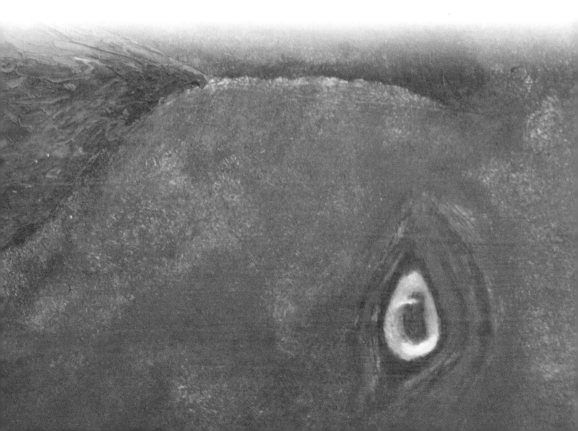

WHAT IS THE MEANING OF THIS MATZOH?

Matzoh is a symbol of the simple bread of poverty. The matzoh reminds us of the great haste in which the Israelites fled from Egypt. As we read in the Torah: "They baked unleavened cakes of the dough since they had been driven out of Egypt and could not delay."

In ancient times, the Israelites lived in the desert, eating simple foods. For one week each year the matzoh becomes the symbol of those days when people had little, reminding us that our lives are about much more than the material things we have or own.

We are commanded to eat matzoh on the first night of Passover and to rid ourselves of chometz – all bread and leavened food products made from wheat, barley, rye, oats and spelt–for the entire holiday. Though we are prohibited from eating these grains during Passover, we are also commanded to eat Matzoh – flour and water baked so quickly that it does not ferment or rise – at the Seder.

The flat, unleavened matzoh represents humility. Matzoh is not "enriched" with oil, sugar, honey or other things. Only by acknowledging our own shortcomings and looking to a higher wisdom, can we free ourselves from the arrogance and self-centeredness within our own hearts.

WHAT IS THE MEANING OF THIS MAROR?

We eat the maror, or bitter herbs, to remind ourselves that the Egyptians embittered the lives of our people. As we read: "And they made their lives bitter with hard labor at mortar and brick and in all sorts of drudgery in the field; and they ruthlessly imposed all the tasks upon them."

Even today, oppression remains in the world, and we are meant to taste its bitterness recalling these words : "You shall not oppress a stranger, for you know the feelings of the stranger, having yourselves been strangers in Egypt. When strangers reside with you in your land, you shall not wrong them...You shall love them as yourself, for you were strangers in Egypt. You shall rejoice before God with your son and daughter...and the stranger, and the orphan, and the widow in your midst. Always remember that you were slaves in Egypt."

As we eat the bitter herbs, we are reminded to remove any bitterness from our own lives, for bitterness will kill even sooner than death. If we become used to bitterness in our lives, it is very hard to ever leave it behind.

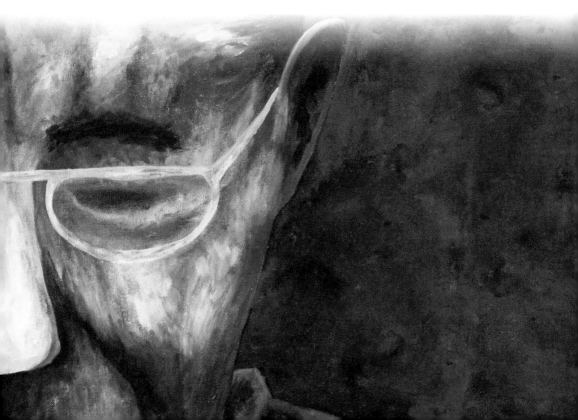

THE CUP OF DELIVERANCE - The Second Cup of Wine

Our wine glasses are raised as we recite the following:

We raise our cups as we recall the second promise of liberation to the people of Israel. Let us glorify God who performed these miracles for our ancestors and for us. Let us rejoice at the wonder of our deliverance from bondage to freedom, from servitude to redemption. Hallelujah. We praise God who has delivered us and our ancestors from Egypt and brought us here this night to eat matzoh and maror. Our God and God of our ancestors, help us celebrate future holidays and festivals in peace and in joy.

בָּרוּךְ אַתָּה יהוה אֱלֹהֵינוּ מֶלֶךְ הָעוֹלָם בּוֹרֵא פְּרִי הַגָּפֶן.

Baruch Atah Adonai, Eloheinu Melech ha-olam, borei p'ri ha-gafen.

**Praised be thou, O Lord Our God, King of the Universe,
who creates the fruit of the vine!**

All drink the entire second cup of wine

RAHATZ - Washing the Hands

Before we eat, let us wash our hands and say together:

בָּרוּךְ אַתָּה יהוה אֱלֹהֵינוּ מֶלֶךְ הָעוֹלָם אֲשֶׁר קִדְּשָׁנוּ
בְּמִצְוֹתָיו וְצִוָּנוּ עַל נְטִילַת יָדָיִם.

**Baruch Atah Adonai, Eloheinu Melech ha-olam,
asher kidshanu b'mitzvo-tav, v'tzivanu al n'tee-lat yada-yim.**

**We praise You God who hallows our lives with commandments
and has granted us the privilege of your blessings of food
after the washing of the hands.**

A pitcher of water with basin and towel is again passed around to all guests

MOTZI - A Blessing for Bread

We are now coming to the Seder meal. As we ordinarily begin with the breaking of bread, we begin tonight with the breaking of matzoh. We recite two blessings; first the regular blessing for bread, then a special one for matzoh.

The upper and middle piece of the three matzot are broken and distributed among the group as we recite together

בָּרוּךְ אַתָּה יהוה אֱלֹהֵינוּ מֶלֶךְ הָעוֹלָם הַמּוֹצִיא לֶחֶם מִן הָאָרֶץ

**Baruch Atah Adonai, Eloheinu Melech ha-olam,
ha-motzi lechem min ha-aretz.**

We praise You, God, who brings forth bread from the earth.

MATZOH - A Special Blessing for Matzoh

בָּרוּךְ אַתָּה יהוה אֱלֹהֵינוּ מֶלֶךְ הָעוֹלָם אֲשֶׁר קִדְּשָׁנוּ בְּמִצְוֹתָיו וְצִוָּנוּ עַל אֲכִילַת מַצָּה.

**Baruch Atah Adonai, Eloheinu Melech ha-olam,
asher kidshanu b'mitzvo-tav v'tzivanu al a-chilat matzoh**

**We praise You, God, who hallows our lives with commandments,
and enjoins us to partake in eating matzoh.**

Each participant eats a portion of the two matzohs

MAROR - A Blessing for the Bitter Herbs

We now dip our food for a second time. Each of us will take a bit of the maror, the bitter herb, and dip it into the haroset – a mixture of chopped apples, nuts, wines and spices. We acknowledge that life is bittersweet. The sweet taste of haroset symbolizes that no matter how bitter and dark the present appears, we should look forward to better days. As we remember our ancestors, this is a time to be appreciative of everything we have; a time to be grateful for all the gifts we have been given.

All recite the following together:

בָּרוּךְ אַתָּה יהוה אֱלֹהֵינוּ מֶלֶךְ הָעוֹלָם אֲשֶׁר קִדְּשָׁנוּ
בְּמִצְוֹתָיו וְצִוָּנוּ עַל אֲכִילַת מָרוֹר.

**Baruch Atah Adonai, Eloheinu Melech ha-olam,
asher kidshanu b'mitzvo-tav, v'tzivanu al a-chilat maror.**

**We praise God who hallows our lives with commandments,
and enjoins us to eat the bitter herbs.**

Each participant eats the bitter herbs along with the sweet haroset

KOREKH

On Passover, Hillel, the head of the Rabbinic academy in Jerusalem two thousand years ago, combined the pesach, matzoh and maror and ate them together, so he might observe the commandment exactly: "They shall eat the Pesach lamb offering with matzoh and maror together." The destruction of the Temple by the Romans brought an end to animal sacrifices, so our sandwich today is made only with matzoh and maror. We will now eat the bitter herbs sandwiched between two pieces of matzoh.

Break two pieces of the bottom matzoh, and use it to make a sandwich with maror

It is customary to begin the Passover meal with hard-boiled eggs flavored with salt water. The egg is symbolic of new life, and of hope; the salt water, a symbol of tears. Eggs, unlike other foods, harden when they are cooked, symbolic of our faith being tempered and hardened by the forces of our history.

May we reflect on our lives this year and soften our hearts to those around us. Another year has passed since we gathered at the Seder table and we are once again reminded that life is fleeting. We are reminded to use each precious moment wisely so that no day will pass without bringing us closer to some worthy achievement as we all take a moment to be aware of how truly blessed and fortunate we are.

Our faith gives us many holidays to celebrate throughout the year and they are all times for self reflection, gently guiding us to a better path in life. We are each given a chance to reflect on our past year; to think about where we have been and how we will live our lives in the year to come. We reaffirm our commitment to lead good and meaningful lives, making peace wherever we go.

SHULCHAN OREKH

The Meal is Served

TZAFUN - The Afikoman is Found and Eaten

Toward the end of the meal, the children look for the afikoman, which has been hidden. Since neither the meal nor the Seder can be concluded before everyone has eaten a piece of it, whoever finds the afikoman is given a reward. Nothing is eaten after the afikoman, so that the matzoh may be the last food tasted. This custom of hiding the afikoman is not found in early Haggadot and was probably added as a device to keep up the interest of young children who might otherwise become bored with the ceremony.

In temple times the Passover sacrifice was eaten at the end of the meal, when everyone was full. In remembrance of this, we each partake of the afikoman as the very last food to be eaten at our Seder.

Eat the afikoman

BAREKH - The Blessing After the Meal

Traditionally, a series of prayers and blessings after eating are now recited in Hebrew. Together we say:

We have eaten this Passover meal as a free people and we give thanks to God for his many blessings. Preserve us in life, sustain us with good and honorable work and make us worthy. Bless this home, this table, and all assembled here; may all our loved ones share our blessings.

THE CUP OF REDEMPTION - The Third Cup of Wine

Fill the third cup of wine

Together we take up the third cup of wine, now recalling the third divine promise to the people of Israel: "And I will redeem you with an outstretched arm."

בָּרוּךְ אַתָּה יהוה אֱלֹהֵינוּ מֶלֶךְ הָעוֹלָם בּוֹרֵא פְּרִי הַגָּפֶן.

Baruch Atah Adonai, Eloheinu Melech ha-olam, borei p'ri ha-gafen.

We now drink the third cup of wine

WE EXPLAIN THE CUP OF ELIJAH

The wine glasses are refilled – including the wine glass for Elijah,
which is now filled to the top

We fulfill our obligations to God through Torah study and prayer but also through our daily lives – how we make a living, how we conduct our affairs, how we reach out to those around us.

In the center of our table is a cup of wine called "Kos Eliyahu"; the cup of Elijah. Elijah was a Prophet who declared that he would return in each generation disguised as a poor or oppressed person. He would come to people's doors to see how he would be treated in order to determine if the people were ready to be redeemed.

Let us now open the door for Elijah!

A child is sent to open the door

HALLEL

THE CUP OF ACCEPTANCE - The Fourth Cup of Wine

Hallel is a recitation in Hebrew of Psalms. This is the time to once again give thanks. It is a time of singing and of praise. We are to love God with all our hearts, with all our souls and with all our might and to diligently teach our children the Torah commandments, speaking of them daily and keeping them close to our minds and close to our hearts. Just as the fringes on our prayer shawls are meant to remind us of our bond, we are reminded that our Jewish identity should not be kept on the fringes of our lives, but brought close to our hearts, enveloping all that we do.

As our Seder comes to an end, we drink the fourth cup of wine. This cup recalls our covenant with God and the tasks that await us as a people called to service.

בָּרוּךְ אַתָּה יהוה אֱלֹהֵינוּ מֶלֶךְ הָעוֹלָם בּוֹרֵא פְּרִי הַגָּפֶן.

Baruch Atah Adonai, Eloheinu Melech ha-olam, borei p'ri ha-gafen.

All drink the fourth cup of wine

NIRTZAH

Our Seder now ends. Next year in Jerusalem. Next year may all men and women everywhere be free!

THE SEDER - The Second Night

Traditionally, the Seder is repeated on the second night of the holiday. Following the commandment to tell the story, participants may wish to take turns reading chapters one through fourteen from the book of Exodus, while eating matzoh, drinking wine and reclining over dinner. Questions are encouraged.